T0132161

Walking Still

*Poetic Reflections of Friends, Family, Life,
and Love*

TAAJ

iUniverse, Inc.
New York   Bloomington

iUniverse books may be ordered through booksellers or by contacting:

iUniverse
1663 Liberty Drive
Bloomington, IN 47403
www.iuniverse.com
1-800-Authors (1-800-288-4677)

ISBN: 978-1-4401-9865-6 (sc)
ISBN: 978-1-4401-9864-9 (ebook)
ISBN: 978-1-4401-9863-2 (dj)

Printed in the United States of America

iUniverse rev. date: 01/25/2010

This book is dedicated to
My best *friend*, closest *family member*, partner in *life*, my true
love,
HAQ

All photos by Shaheed J. Qaasim

Contents

Poetic Reflections of Family

Poetic Reflections of Life

Poetic Reflections of Love

Preface

Have you ever taken a journey without packing a suitcase or physically moving from one place to another? Well, *Walking Still: Poetic Reflections of Friends, Family, Life, and Love* is that type of journey. These poems examine the emotive journey that each of us experiences from just living. We naturally reflect on our life experiences. We attempt to capture these experiences visually in many ways: digital frames, photo albums, and even in shoeboxes. These images help us to hold onto treasured memories that otherwise could be lost. We also attempt to reflect on our experiences through conversations, in our dreams, and in the arts, such as music and dance. Basically, any way we can.

A photograph only captures a moment in time, memories in dreams are distortions of the true experiences, conversations invite other perceptions that may change our own, and attempts to memorialize our experiences through music and dance are limited by artistic ability. Nevertheless, we continue to walk through our thoughts to relive treasured experiences or learn valuable lessons.

Reflection on our experiences is basic to us as humans; we are driven by ideas, purpose, and thoughts of our past. The ability to reflect on who we are allows us to grow and develop as people, to have empathic thoughts toward others, and to think critically about life or, in other words, to become courageous, compassionate, and competent. *Walking Still: Poetic Reflections of Friends, Family, Life, and Love* consists of reflections about life's experiences that allowed me to grow as a friend, wife/mother, teacher/poet, and woman. Simply put, to enjoy living by sharing experiences through words.

In this book, I show you how starting with the safer reflections of others will lead to examining the relations of family, which are much closer to home. Once we can look back at those close relationships, it opens us up to the true journey of self-discovery, where we can examine our innermost feelings about the difficult life struggles. Whether we express it in poetry, in journals, to our loved ones, or just quietly to ourselves, moments of walking still make it possible for us to still walk. It is the act of self-expression that truly sets us free.

I believe *Walking Still* will encourage many of you to reflect on your life's experiences and provide joy and comfort to you. It is my hope that some of my poetic reflections speak to you personally.

Taaj

Poetic Reflections of Friends

Everyone needs at least one friend whom they can trust with his or her stories. Life's lessons are learned from making mistakes and sharing what we have learned with others. It is easy to share the comedies and even the love stories, but tragedies are difficult to bequeath to other people.

Friends have inspired the following poetic reflections. Through their stories, I have learned ways to lift myself above life's pain and heartbreak. I have a better understanding of how experiences allow us to heal and transform challenges into opportunities that will ultimately improve our lives and relationships. It is my sincere desire to honor these narratives shared by friends through poetry, while encouraging others to share their experiences in a similar manner.

A Friend ...

A friend sent two poems,
Reaching deep below the surface,
Not skipping across the water
Like goslings in surprise
Or dunking briefly for morsels.

She sent words that submerge
Into the lower depths like a submarine
As its crew scrubs out the belly
Where it's lonely, dark, inescapable,
So courageous.

A friend sent two poems
That spoke of stories, evoking
Reality with ebbs and tides,
Companion to honesty
And like a mighty pelican,
Her words make me dive
With determination
Not to come up empty.

Wishbone

A gift of a "wishbone"
For changing age,
She picked up a box,
Opened it up
And really,
There was the bone,
End to end; marrow stuck,
Representing hopeful intent
Sucked of flesh,
Gnawed of skin.
Scrubbed of grease,
Said was clean.

Just a piece of skeleton,
Was it a gag?
A laughable rib?
Not these fowl limbs
From friend to friend.

This trinket was accepted
Without a gasp.
In fact, when asked,
The wish was made
On molded carcass,
Broken in half
For potential order
From familiar structure,
I sat in amazement
That this illogical present
Was actually given
As an eventful relic.

With a yuck shiver,
Of all the nerve!
My birthday's next
In a relationship
Far less intimate,
Perhaps an exit
Receiving bone from chicken.

Broken Fidelity

Infidelity recycles itself,
Parents getting treats from tricks,
Destroying their offspring's security,
Thinking what children don't know
Won't hurt them.

But these natural beings
Believe in normal things.
They're not foolish,
Observing what parents are doing
Lying to the ones
They should love.
Too many bedtime stories
Were never read
And only one tucked them in.
Staged illusions
Endowed sons and daughters
With polygamous futures.

Smoky memories of failed good intentions
Are now worn like family apparitions
Of unicorns who left in the morning
And didn't appear until the next day,
Or fairytale queens lustfully sighing
While kings were away.

Dull recollections of wedded bliss
Held under stale arms,
Between unwashed teeth,
Stuck in uncombed hair.
No need to clean
Where caresses won't be
Or kisses no longer linger
Both now in the streets.

Until the invitations arrive
For the pity parties
Lovers' leftovers are offered
In repentance,
Not fine dining
But enough to stave off starvation.
Kids need to eat,
Mortgages need to get paid,
And to assuage the lonely
For being alone,
Doggy bags are accepted
With the stench of decay
Replacing the romantic fragrance
Of a once healthy marriage.

Weeping children
Who don't understand their anxiety,
Knowing something is wrong,
But can't call it by name.
Their potential for "happy ever after"
Shaved off
As one parent condones
While the other does it,
Both pretending
Children aren't learning
Love means betrayal
And betrayal is expected.

But the forked tongues
Have poisoned the honorable ones
And the venom soaked with disgrace
Is like waste,
Floating where it was conceived
It stinks!

Cheating should have ended
Before it began
Or begin to end
Before it got started
Or started to end
What should never have been.
And with false spousal regrets
They attempt to flush the mess.

Knowing it's a matter of time
That the head will be hard
And the beaver will be wet.

Aesthetic Clarity

Female Color,
Breathless!
Shaded in earthy pastels,
Rich black with undertones
Of purple, delineated
Blue or red
Hershey's kisses
Soft gradient browns,
Pinks, ivory,
Porcelain white
Painted figures of past
Love affairs
Everywhere.

Woman Shape
Speechless!
Impressionistic,
Flat back
Aligned with bottom
Middle canal
Or backward
"S," under exaggerated,
Slightly round,
Dimpled where accentuated.

Feminine pillars,
Expressionistic!
Appendages
Meeting head, feet, and hands
Long, sleek, or short,
For dance, romance, nurturance,
Perfection at any age.

Holy Grail, private places,
Temptress!
Orifices,
Eyes, mouth, inner lips,
View the soul,
Feel it, exist in,
Enter at risk if uncommitted,
Specific beauty
Acquired taste,
Requires class,
Desires only art appreciators.

Apparent

Lack of discernment
Is desolate.
Vision anatomically
Lost,
Eyes impotent
The dunes swirling,
Grainy winds
Making the traveler
A blind wanderer
Feet bleeding for the road
Less traveled.
Can there be clarity?
Yes!
A compass
Constructed from life
Where cancerous cells
Died.
There is a choice,
An arrow that points
Downward
Toward pain
Or upward
Toward the cure.
Self-love is an
Obvious direction.

Iceberg and the Lighthouse

A young boy with a tender soul
Became lost beneath the deep snow,
From storms of youth with bitter cold
That eventually caused the blizzard.

The turbulence reigned far too long,
As ice moved slowly and spread beyond
Male adolescent endurance.

A glacier stressed of polarized drugs
Decimated the familial structure,
Breaking in half, leaving instead
An iceberg against the current.

But a lighthouse in the distance dauntless,
A tower not deceived by the image
Of an obvious tip viewed as the trouble
Was aware of the hidden bottom.

The mast threw light down below
To reveal the stronger substance,
Faith, maternal dedication, viability,
A foundation to stop the mass destruction
Of perpetual life disease.

With the lighthouse's illumination,
The depth is fully viewed,
For the iceberg to scour his potential
To turn turf into fortitude.

Bound in Circles

Her eyes sunk deep into her head,
Circles with shadows of disillusionment,
Life was to go the other way.
He was born to wear silly grins.
No one was meant to be like him,
Her only child, her one true love
Found webs of entanglement.

The man he was suppose to be
Is snared and strangled in misery.
Holding his mother captured,
Their webs are bound together,
Circular traps until unwrapped,
Allowing them both to imagine.

Aging

An osprey bathed on the beach.
Two surfers rode the waves.
Nearby, several seals played,
She walked, soaked in sand, bare feet.
None of them looked her way
Or saw her smile that day.

Did they choose to ignore her?
Perhaps the rooftop was too white
Or they just didn't see
Because the canvass was too dark.
Once, when the lady was younger,
Surfers whistled in delight.
Forget the dear osprey, at least
The seals should have barked.

Survivor

A girl child lifted above the bed,
Crying for someone to save her soul
As he did his business below,
Trust raining from her heart,
Telling her it was none of her business
And not to tell anyone,
It wasn't their right to know,
Only his,
To do what he wanted; to his daughter.

Her eyes formed unlit sockets
No glimmer of hope,
The girl child or the soul.
Apertures that held all that he did
Without her permission,
Losing dreams of a future beau
Doing the same thing
For infatuation.

Replaced fantasy of ever getting it right
With flesh burning from the touch of shame,
Tears sizzling into blistering skin
That melts into the incestuous plight
Of bed sheets, changed by the real wife,
A woman who lost her sight
In her own family of pain.

So as the virgin floats down from the ceiling
And merges with the broken ghost,
They wait for daylight,
Planning how to save their siblings,
Vowing to protect their innocence
But gone already, was the purity.

Because they were not caregivers,
Only two adults consumed by chores
They could not ignore
Staining the sheets at night
Cleaning the beds at dawn.

Schoolhouse Blues

There's nothing to learn
From padlocks on doors,
Washed-out budgets,
Stale tissue lining floors
Where kids once migrated
Are now brown corridors
Of scat from rats
Roaming the halls,
Self-appointed janitors
Keeping the building inhabited.

Rodents!
Parents!
Adolescents!
A shrine for education
Now a shed for crystal meth.
Medicating their evictions
With a stimulus package
Not depleted yet.

But it won't clean the trash
Or bring the teachers back,
'Cause no one endures
Anymore,
Now that welfare
Goes to the rich
Instead of the poor.

Keeping It Real

"You ain't no girl no mo,"
Momma told me so.

Even though
She knew I thought I was
Just too afraid not to be one,
Still talking high pitched
Like I don't know nothin'.

Once cute
With dimples front and back,
Stomach flat,
Chest at attention.

My giggles continuous,
Long after cuteness was gone.
What were smiles of admiration
Is banter now for being ridiculous?
A woman who didn't
Leave her youth behind
After it drooped from gravitation.

So Momma chided,
"You ain't no girl no mo."

The Magic Belongs to Me

You don't own my spell.
You've been a
Heartache,
Headache,
Backbreak;
Don't take any lovemaking kind of spell to me.
But you don't own my spell.
You can't even spell it, because you can't
Feel it,
Touch it,
Taste it,
Only waste it.
Being nice is too nice for you.
You don't own my spell.

Because no one taught you to
Cuddle when it's warm,
Snuggle when it's cool,
Just sex when it's hot,
And you only do that to be a spell spoiler.
But I am a spell caster
And the next star of my spell
Baby, won't be you!

Because you made me
Whine in the summertime,
Cuss and fuss too many times.
My mind been twisted
Around a dream with no fruition.
My heart been thumping
To a drum made of glass,
Splintering sharp pointed edges of pain
Into the very fiber of a spell
I called love,
You called convenience,
I called happiness,

You called "Only your way,"
I called family,
You called, "Get out of my way."
But you are not my spell anymore.
I gave you the power,
Today I'm taking it back.
I'm not asking you to give it back,
It wasn't yours when I gave it.
Spells only belong to those who create the Magic!

Poetic Reflections of Family

Stories shared by friends have allowed doors to open deeper, more meaningful memories that although sometimes painful are, nonetheless, an important journey. This journey helps us to connect to our personal family narratives.

Family naturally inspires poetic reflections; these are the most treasured people in our lives. They hold our deepest love and have the greatest impact on us. The diversity in families makes it a complicated process toward achieving cooperation, cohesiveness, and just plain peace. But we never give up trying. The following poetic reflections of my family became a therapeutic exercise. A family member inspired each poem, and like my friends, these poems are narratives about real people. Additionally, these are shared experiences with my most beloved relatives. It is my hope that these poems inspire you to find poetic expressions that will set you free.

Cleansing

I want to pour all of me out.
I want to spill all over concrete.
So no one dare wipe me up,
And if they dare try,
Let their knuckles bleed
For just not letting me be.
Please, please
Let me pour,
Until I'm empty.

When Daddies Were Home

Afternoons were familiar,
The way the sunrays dropped
On the dull concrete
Like fool's gold, it sparkled.
The click clack of the city's rhythms,
Mixed with laughter
Street beats that made kids skip
To nursery rhymes.
Smells that caused long whiffs,
Impossible with open eyes,
No need to see sweet potatoes, chicken, and greens
Or peach cobbler
That gave us tiny tickles.
We disappeared at dawn
Didn't reappear until dusk.
Playing was as natural
As boys chasing the prettiest girls
Or always being warned,
"Don't hang with those bad kids,"
Delinquents that chewed gum
Or threw wet tissue in restrooms.
Those were the times when mamas yelled,
"Stop! Get in the house."

Our youth had a different color.
Life glowed with a happy green hue
As if the lens in our eyes were mixed
With sunny yellow and sky blue.
We were superstitious,
Afraid to step on sidewalk cracks
Or black cats
If they crossed our path,
Or to walk under ladders
Knowing that fate
May deprive us of the Schwinn,
A doll that peed, scooter or skates.

Just urban urchins
Talking in code secrets,
Blood mixed brothers and sisters
Because the real ones were pests.
Those were the days
We didn't worry about HIV or hepatitis,
Just our kid dreams.
We were Jacob Lawrence's paintings
Turning long-legged somersaults;
His visions,
Until our mama called a second time,
"Get in the house."

We knew she meant it.
This time she meant business,
Which was no fun.
Belt, twig, an ironing cord,
We had no choice
But to return
Calling out in our "John Boy" repetition,
"See ya,"
"See ya, Nedra," "See ya, Silas, Tony, and Renee."

Daddies greeted us
Each day after work
Watching black-and-white TVs,
Listening to Billie's moans
On LPs,
Present!
Never absent.

We washed our hands
A spot on a face
As supper was prepared
In kitchens for every member
Like soldiers in a mess hall,
We were seen, not heard.
But it didn't matter
As we fed dogs named Foxy and Max under the table,

Retreating into bunks
Stuffed with love and tall tales
And bedtime stories from big mamas and nanas,
A lullaby called "Summertime"
With wistful smiles
Telling of their childhood
 Tinted in blue.

Those were the days
Families were more than a house, street, or name.
A community was a neighborhood.
Mamas and Babas raised us in villages,
Taught us to read, think, and obey
But most of all,
Allowed us innocence.
So, "as He laid us down to sleep,"
We remembered,
Like Dorothy,
In her world of blue sky and yellow sunlight,
She was right,
 When she said every Xmas night,
        "There's … no … place … like … home
        "There's … no … place … like … home
        "There's … no … place … like … home"

He's home!

Natalia's Butterfly

The energy above my head
Asked me to look up
I saw you fluttering over me
And beneath you was beauty,
Not me but you.
Perhaps you thought
I was beautiful too?

19 Months

She's rose petals bouncing in spring water,
Blowing fresh air kisses into northwest wind.
She's sparkling eye stares with curious recognition,
Entering in a soulful door, a first time visitant,
She waved.

Did she sense the love from a matron's heart?
Was it the joy ringing from appetent ears?
In sweet anticipation did she hear,
 "There's Grammy's baby"?
She smiled.

She's an enactment of parents' preparation
And I reached out gratuitous arms
In absolute amazement!

Dinky's Apples

I had an aunt named Dinky.
She wore apples
In my eyes,
The larger ones
Worn on her cheeks,
The sweeter ones inside.

Wavy hair, golden skin,
Curvaceous as a pear
She laughed, joked, pranced around
And danced like Martha Graham.

Until the day, an accident
Took her joy far away.
She thought she lost her good looks,
Which stole her marriage and faith.

With lesser body, brokenhearted,
She buried her dreams away
And flooded her soul with alcohol
To keep the ghosts at bay.

But even weaker, broken, buried,
Motherly love, she maintained
Pride in family, whatever she had,
Where once, someone called vain.

She was "sweet auntie" of my youth,
Distant relative of my older age
Someone I loved then, still love now,
Though I may never see again.

If I'm blessed, and if He ordains,
I've one prayer for God above,
Put Dinky's apples back on her face
And show her how ripe they are.

Crying Wisdom

My mama said crying is good
And she wasn't talking to girls, but boys.
That's why the boys I know shed tears
And they aren't boys no more, but men.

My mama said crying grows wings
And not the kind on the backyard sparrows
But the kind that catch fallen queens,
Wings with muscle, bone, and fiber.

My mama said crying builds homes
And not those with wood, brick, and mortar,
But shelters that withstand challenge and trouble,
Understanding the "how come" of tomorrow.

So I say all men should just start crying,
Embrace what is naturally inside.
Tears were there on your first birthday
Yes, they'll be there when you pass away.

You don't need these events
To show this expression,
Some of the most secure humans
Like it and do it.

You know them, love them, and respect them
And they aren't called children, girls, or women.

Mama's Soliloquy

I was a roach under his foot.
Long before we were wed
I knew he disrespected within.
I married him anyway.

This boy riddled with heroin,
An aphrodisiac that skewed his pain
And distanced him from spousal shame
Of his actions
And of his father
Who didn't love his son.

So he forced his fists down on my face
Because I did
What his daddy should have.
I loved him every day
Until I drowned my sorrows
In 80-proof bottles
In order for me to stay.

God became my lover and friend
And I was baptized
Removing "my man's" privilege
To continue the damage he did.

Before he died,
Forgiveness came as his repentance.
After all, I was a saved woman,
Not a roach.

Cruel Rhapsody

She lay under the table
Like an old dishrag or
The Raggedy Ann doll that
She gave her child.
Didn't dare move, afraid,
More than her pride was broken,
Until she felt the small hands
Of her little girl
Under the furniture,
Touching the tangible bruises.
So she mustered the strength
To lift her arms,
Embracing with warmth,
Saying as sweetly as she might,
"Everything will be all right."
And her daughter, who was then
No more than seven,
Said, "Mama, why did Daddy beat
You with a belt?"
As tears were choked back
In protective strain,
She decided not to explain
It wasn't a belt, but the dog's chain.

Blue without Yellow

Chartreuse, lime, olive, teal, moss, jade,
Army, Persian, Pine, Midnight greens,
Not shades for her brown skin.
With violence, a sanguineous color
On a lesser level
Semblance
Of a burning forest,
Not a color to live in.

Once, when she was five years old,
Sitting in a dark corridor,
With star-shaped splatters
On face and arms,
Slime not algae
Oozing from a gallon can
After Daddy, an angry man
Covered Mama's hair and head,
A vessel, receiving libation.

Drip, drip, drip

Paint spilling off clothes
To a little girl's legs,
Asparagus hue, turning red
As he dragged
The female leprechaun
Into another cave.

The child remained in her star-
Studded stunned galaxy.

Waiting … Waiting … Waited …

I haven't worn green since.

Grand Divas

Two grand divas,
Big Mama and Mama Eva,
An overture, an interlude,
Big Mama resides in my mama's eyes.
Mama Eva intervened in my daddy's life.
Two grand divas live inside me
One, I'll call classical melody
The other free jazz beats.

Mama Eva was a prima donna,
White linen, lace, scrub with polish,
Conventional, traditional as a recitative opera
Brown leather chairs, mahogany wood
Ceramic walls, crooked fingers on hands so smooth,
An aria of fresh air not just for the classic
But understanding of the aesthetic,
She gave me gifts, I call the basics,
Smart children, clean home, a healthy marriage.

Big Mama a real jazz songstress,
She lulled me to sleep like Billie Holiday's whines.
I still remember her improvisations,
Especially the one she called "Summertime."
Even now, her oratorio is sacred.
I learned from her my love for lyrics.
When I was young she seemed
So much older, but as I got older,
She seemed so much younger.
I will never know the cause of her death.
Unlike Mama Eva's rheumatoid arthritis,
As my life story grows increasingly,
I know its poetry Big Mama gave to me.

Two grand divas, one purely warm,
The other warmly cool.
Both gave notes and chords made of their tunes,
The low sounds of history,
And high sounds of legacy
Infused together
Crescendo, my destiny!

A Grandmother's Plea

She resembles desegregation,
Open borders,
Dismantling of miscegenation.
People ask the racial question,
"What is she?"
Putting her in boxes
Of common binary guesses.

Is she white or black?
As if people are painted in neutrals
Instead of a rainbow spectrum.
They eventually acquiesce
To the obvious,
She is a child of color
And surely "at risk,"
As if white is colorless
And exists in a sanitized vacuum.

With her mama they say,
"She is mixed."
Struggle to place her on the census list.
With her papi they say,
"She is Hispanic.
"Wonder if she speaks English?"
Believing as a child of color
She must be "at risk."

She is the *nieta* of Peruvian immigrants.
Her *abuelos* come from the coastal city of Lima
And the mountain town of Cuzco.
She's visited the ruins of Machu Picchu.
Her grammie and grandada are African Americans,
One of the oldest ethnicities in the U.S.

She is American,
She is African,
She is Inca!

But too often,
Too many, see a child of color
Who must be "at risk."

She is black and Latina,
For those who ask the question
"What is she?"
She's a child who can't learn,
A child who won't learn,
Whose parents don't care,
Trapped in economic and social despair.

Here's an adage
We're told to hold dear.
Don't judge a book by its cover,
As teachers don't judge students
By their physical features.
This is called race.
And that is all that it is,
Skin color, hair, and the shapes on the face,
Not potential, cognition, character, or grace.

This child's mother grew up middle class
By standards, her father is successful.
Her mama went to law school,
Papi went to Stanford.
She lives in a large house
Near the beach,
Her room is pink,
It makes her happy.
As a child of color, is she really at risk?

She learned to read
When she was three.

She speaks
Two languages fluently
In dialects when having fun,
Like Quechua
When she was two,
Ebonics, when upset with you.

As a child of color, is she really at risk?

Nevertheless,

She is a child of color and most certainly at risk!

But Ms. Strange,
A kindergarten teacher
With the ironic name,
White, free, over 21
So wonderfully open
Understands
What puts a child at risk.
Prejudice and ignorance!

So she never asked,
Out loud or silently,
"What is she?"
But asked instead,
"What's your name?"

"My name is Kamilah Sade.
"I will be five years old in November,
"I like to read,
"I like Polly Pockets,
"Swimming and chocolate."

This is who she is,
My granddaughter called Mila.

You WILL see her
What will you presume?
What will be your first impression?
Children "at risk" because of their rich complexion
Or a kind, funny, intelligent, active linguist.

Epiphany
I. Stage of Awareness

There's a tap
On my bedroom door
That aroused me from sleep,
Just a soft knock, loud enough to stop my dreams.
Not the first, nor the last, this presence from old
Wakens me once more.

Alas, I realize who you are,
Why you've come.
Oh, my sweet imagination,
Why so long to become
A phantom in clear view,
No longer ghostly in my mind.
You have startled me for the last time,
No longer a vestige bumping in the dark
Requesting my presence.
I'm reaching for a pen
To write down my thoughts.
No need to ask, "Who's there?"
Or "For what?"

For the rest of my existence
I will not exit in slumber,
But arise and uncover
What needs to be expressed
Before dozing into forgetfulness.
Sleep that rejects
The memories that ironically surface
During the very state I must leave.

You are a tenacious companion
Who insists that I write,
Sharing the pain of a once tragic end.

II. Stage of Discovery

Oh, imagination,
You were more than a tap
 When I was a child,
A glowing lady in white
A light touch of comfort.
Then my innocence allowed
You in without shadows,
A fuller form,
A voice of softness
That brought me peace.

Oh, gentle spirit of my youth,
How you lulled me to sleep
Many nights after my parents' fights.
Ancient whispers of days past,
You kept me alive inside the pain.
In my ear you said,
"Mama didn't deserve
The humiliation."

To ignore the screams
That rang throughout the house,
Mama had no rights,
She was Daddy's merchandise.
She had no choice
And it did get worse.
Did Mama's beatings
Take my sister's life?
Not by my father's hands,
But the examples of his demands.

III. Stage of Recovery

My sister was only nineteen.
He was a tall, handsome man
With ebony skin
Like the crows
That would eventually feast
Around her grave.
He married my sister,
Gave her a child
And when their son was two,
Took my sister's soul.

She had no choice,
When he locked her behind
An iron gate,
Officers asked,
"What made your husband irate?"
When her face
Received twenty stitches,
She was told to ask for repentance.
She hid in order to stay alive,
Until the day our grandmother died.

I tapped on her apartment door
To take her home,
It creaked open and
Revealed the stench of death.
I tracked it to a bathroom and
Found this young sibling of mine,
Face down in a tub,
Wasting from a monster's crime
And her two-year-old infant,
With his tear-stained face,
Pointing, "Mommy's wet."
This child had no choice
And still it got worse.

No justice for the victims,
The husband disappeared,
Nephew with him.

So the taps at my door
For thirty years or more,
Was my imagination that needed to turn true,
Dreams needing to become memories,
A tragic end that changed my reality
As this story is long overdue.
I dig my fingers into my eyes,
Pushing tears to the other side,
My pulsating heart says, girl just cry.
Keep the door open, afterward write,
Or what was the point of healing?

Splendid Image

I know a sculptured face that makes me sigh.
It reminds me of my own, the same jawline
But with the "it" factor, different yet alike.
For example

Squared off to make it masculine,
Bones sharply aligned
From temples to where it tapers,
Not soft like yellow apples,
Perpendicular angles, sharp edges,
Shadowed cheeks,
Photographic art piece
Displaying definition.

Deep eyes
In front of sprint mind
Marathon when listening,
Shaded by a brow line,
Clearly Cro-Magnon,
Touch of Neanderthal,
Symmetrical lips,
Full for audacious kiss,
Angst, a maternal elegy.

Instead, a mouth,
Anatomically perfect
For quick intellect
That flows in a whim
As argumentative debate
Demonstrates critical taste
Of a technical caste,
Though charismatic.

Amused devil's advocate,
No burden to boredom,
Tongue-in-cheek wit
Fitted in emotive vulnerability,
Perhaps necessary for such beauty.

Splendor that struts from
Athleticism to competition.
Dancing out Ella's articulations
And Armstrong's improvisations
Sensual squints to the rhythms
Or tongue hanging drags
From musical interpretations.

Yes, I know a face that makes me sigh
It reminds me of my own, the same jawline
But with the "it" factor, different yet alike.

Wished I had known its full potential!

Natalia's Curls, Kamilah's Waves

My granddaughters have their own brands,
One is one, the other is seven.
Natalia's curls are golden bronze,
Kamilah's waves turn reddish brown,
Sunhats holding hidden curls,
Spring rain causing waves to twirl
Uniquely different from each other
But sweetly similar for first cousins.
Baby seeking autonomy,
Schoolgirl forming identity,
Receiving snuggly curls from the oldest
And bye-bye waves from the youngest.
Still alike, because both are stubborn,
Making water waves in swimming pools
Or crayon curls on Winnie Pooh,
Lips curling when blowing bubbles,
Hands waving when they're busted,
Natalia kissing curled up Shadow,
Kamilah waving finger at Magic.
These are the pets they adore
The first is a cat, the other a Labrador.
"Yah-Yah" reaching up for birds,
"Mila" hanging butterflies in room of turquoise,
Sniffing the fragrance of floral petals
Or drawing them on "I love you" Post-its.
Memories in captured photos
Visited in this poetry,
Living in my soul
As the self-anointed poetic sage
I'll remember these days when old
As Natalia's curls and Kamilah's waves.

She's Called Missy

Bright smile
Statuesque beauty
Requiring presence
For love.

Shaved head for
Mother's health
A faithful, powerful
Daughter.

A cherished niece
In my heart
Near or distant
I've heard you.

Message delivered!

Yes, you're treasured
Love, protected
Perceptions, reflections
Does matter.

As your father's oldest sister,
Woman to woman,
Senior to junior,
May our lives stay

Inseparable!

The Making of a Girl

Make a girl the camera, not the photograph.
Make her a plant in a pot, not a flower in a vase.
Keep a girl a runner, don't tell her to sit.
Keep her a thinker, not just articulate.
Watch her compose, not just sing.
Watch her in sports, instead of shopping,
In other words play games, don't daydream.
Make her a noble fir, not the ornaments
Or Transformer not the Barbie doll.
Why an apparition,
Disfigured, deformed?
CEO, not the assistant,
GPS, not Blu-ray recorder,
The Diner instead of the Cook
Or Master Chef instead of Sous,
The Labrador retriever
Not the Persian cat,
Let her be a caterpillar or butterfly,
Yes, Implementer or Visionary.
Hand not Glove
Head not Hat
Luna Beam
Not Sunset
Hero not Victim
Friend not Foe
Especially to another ingénue
Self-defense is feminine
So reinforce strength but also muscle,
Instead of Secretary of State
Envision President
Make her global
She's already domestic.
Fearless Leader
Not the Peacemaker
A Sprinter

Not a Pacemaker
High tide not low
Not the Hummingbird,
But Eagle, white hooded, if possible
A Bitch, without saying the word
If it means she loves
Self more than a him or her.
Don't insist that she is
Something she's not
For conventions, traditions,
Or religious doctrine.
You are wasting your time
With someone on loan
Her final decisions,
Are her own.
Just instill compassion,
Intelligence; encourage
Education and experiences,
Travel, languages, cultural
Diversity, anti-bias that means,
Skills to fight her own prejudice.
Don't expect perfection, only
Self-regulation. Mommy
Let her see you kiss your
Reflection, and Daddy, make
Sure you are kissing Mommy.
Do these things for her development
And as a woman,
She'll compete and achieve,
Find her own spiritual gifts.
She represents one half of our
Planet. Perhaps
She'll find the cure
For cancer. So don't be
Afraid because she's your daughter,
She's female, woman, an indestructible nature.

Poetic Reflections of Life

Life is about everything we do; it's all around, and even death falls into this category. The themes are endless. I have chosen some topics that tend to peak curiosity, such as nature, aging, and life's challenges. The following poetic reflections examine the beauty of life as well as its skids and collisions. In general, poetic reflections about life allow us to experience our life while it is happening, gives us opportunities to make a difference, and provides avenues for us to lessen our regrets. It is my hope that my poetic reflections about life will help you to examine your own.

Ode to Responsibility

The salted sea reached for me as I walked among debris,
Urban dweller, leaving treasures for fowl with twisted beaks.
The earth on fire, the sky perspires, too weak for permanency
As metallic fleets skin the geese, taking life for nothing.
But as creatures in great urgency they search for vacancies,
A housing lease to live in peace, last chance for decency,
In a place where they can stay with environmental harmony,
Not just for the stricken on the beach, but life entirety.

Oh cries of anguish, the planet is vanishing tragically
Out of the past with the future alas, no longer a necessity.
Who is hoping or even praying for this catastrophe,
Not primal mates or landscapes responding naturally?
But watch me breed and nurse my greed, the rot on living tree,
Ignored confusion and pollution that brought this misery
As trespasser and squatter facing obscurity,
Allowing my home to become eternally filthy.

I snored, sneezed, and snickered away my responsibility,
And called my waste and poor taste post-modernity,
But what I found is tyranny throughout society.
It wasn't those I could not see who were my enemies,
But it was I, the last disease that destroyed the majesty.
If I had but one more chance, enlightened I would be,
I would shape and then create a clean humanity.

Oh fish, birds, beasts, and all things green, you have propriety,
Then I must too, it is for me, and you'll have my sanctity.

Who Killed the Cypress Tree?

Thieves!
Neighbors poisoned
Our cypress tree
Murderers, killers,
Thieves!

Love thy neighbors, vanquished
This act of malice, relinquished
A lake view, behind glass with borders
Where nature breathed,
Masterpiece ruined,
By murderers, killers,
Thieves!

Can't prove it until the dirt is tested
But look out next-door wisteria,
Revengeful penance, when the guilty
Leave for Phoenix,
Vengeance
Murderers, killers,
Thieves!

And then, distraught mate calls
With chainsaw still in hand
While lowering our laurel bush,
Once fifteen feet now ten.
He looked up from his mission,
Hyperventilating, face all flush
And found what he had done
The laurel held a robin's clutch.
Among the sawed-off foliage
Four baby birds now massacred
Stripping our sanctimonious yearning
Atop the neighbors' roof,
The mother fowl a calling,
Murderers, killers,
Thieves!

Perhaps the cypress
Died of natural causes,
Unlike four little robins.

Menopause

Beneath a dewy
Blanket
In fetal position,
Comfort
The official night
Womb
Listening to the
Heart racing,
Stomach churning,
Ears Ringing,
Noise of life passing
Still sounds of existence.

Above is a blink of light.

I Will Not Forsake Thee

Visual expectations,
Fine porcelain statues,
Textured carvings from Cote de Ivoire,
Dull sheen of one from Benin,
Baby's photo, vibrant
Purple mixed with orange and green
On my mother's face, serenity,
Especially with her hands in praise
Granddaughter's tossing windswept waves,
Passionate love of forty years
Kissing away apprehension,
These are the vivid images
Pressed in my mind.

I'm blessed with sight
It's not taken for granted
That which ails me
Is insidiously quiet.
Its young, just an infant
Waiting for substance
To steal what is most valued.

But I must not lose vision,
Committed to preserve thee
One sense not perfect,
But the one that defines me
Thou communicate
How others perceive me.
Thou calm the vertigo
When sleep escapes me,
When my lids are shut
My world sometimes tilts,
But oh, faithful ones,
When you're opened and focused
The horizon becomes horizontal.

Devoutly, I will quench thy thirst
Each drop prescribed will rinse
The pressure off the optic nerve.
Dear eyes do not forsake me
And relax to the river flow,
Let beauty never leave us
Our tears will refresh forever
Like spring water.

Admiration

On the way to see the doctor,
I looked left of my driver's seat,
I saw a map of age on your face.
Thought perhaps,
One day that will be me
As the central canals
Have deepened my cheeks
I wondered when others
Will begin to see
My West coast and East,
Hoping someone admires
My longevity,
As I have yours today.

Sleepless Laments

1.
Sleep evades me,
Escaping my urging,
I beg for an invitation,
But it refuses my presence
I can only wait until I'm worthy
To attend the party.

2.
When I enter the realm of sleep
There is nothing there
But air and movement
Suspending me loosely
In space and I wait to fall,
But I just hang there
Until I awakened and realized
I had finally fallen asleep.

3.
Drifting away in slumber
Is like waiting for that holiday
That you know is going to come
If you can wait long enough,
When it arrives,
You know you'd better
Enjoy every moment
Because it will be a long
Time before the next vacation.

Unrest

In separate beds,
Yours of flower seeds
Facing the trees;
Mines of sheetrock
Buried in weeds,
Pollinating dandelions.

Still wake
Steal sleep
Steel dream.

Chaotic mind
Pieced together,
Peace deprived.

Lyin' in d'lions,
Where the line ends.

Solitude

Alone is not lonely,
Dense with solitude
Solace in self,
Thinking how lonely
Doesn't exist.

Oh, solitude rustle
In between each branch
Upon the trees
Kiss, oh kiss each leaf
Until they sing.

Oh, solitude breathe,
Let air twirl through the
Planks of each fence,
Catching the narrow pathways
With a whistle and whisper.

Oh, solitude sit quietly in my
Mind, and behave yourself.
Be content with whatever
You find. I have been
Waiting for you in and out
Of dreams.

My desire for you
Will never leave.

Quiet Moment

As I slowly open my eyes
To the melodic songs
Of unknown birds
My heart plays
The percussionist beat
To the lyrical refrain
Of my companions.

Beneath the music
It lies
So tantalizing,
I lie still.

Quiet.

Waiting for the sounds
That will interrupt
The moment,
Sending it away
With the sizzle of bacon,
A flush of a toilet,
Or my voice
Saying, "Let's start the day."

Suffering

Suffering is deeper than the surf rolling over high tide
At night when there's nothing to see but darkness,
Anguish with lonely visibility in thin moonlight.

Suffering is as certain as stars dying in the universe,
Light once white, now orange brown as they fade out of sight,
Soaking into the black hole of accidents, mistakes, and
uncontrollable fate.

Suffering is crying out where few ears are brave enough to listen,
Fear of contagion, each saying, "Not me, it is not my turn, but
yours,"
Wounds lying under crusted filter, unreachable from lack of
treatment.

Suffering is unbearable pain scorching already heated bones and
marrow,
Translating torment into wails and screams, instead of quiet pleads
of mercy,
Gentle cries for sleep, prayers for peace, never with thoughts of
recovery.

Suffering is a companion at the beginning, randomly visiting or at
the end.
There is no escaping this accompaniment of life, this unwelcome
visitor,
Sometimes a faithful guest, at others an intruder, nevertheless loyal
and merciless.

Faith

Walking slats,
Thick or thin
Though afraid
Of the depth
In between
Unreachable

Slit in eyes
Of genuine smiles
Closes mine
Faithfully,
Are my prayers
Reachable?

Shall I
Walk the planks
Continuous?

Or

Jump into the
Mayhem
Defenseless?

Trust he'll catch me.

Life

When you live a long life,
When are you prepared
To die?

How many tuna cans
Can you open
Before enough is enough?

Compassion

Lower than the solar plexus,
Down right to the soul,
God did not expect children to suffer.
We know what we know,
When children weep for death,
Did God intend for them
To languish in torment?
Securing their parents' salvation,
Perhaps that's the sin.
Not having faith in … the end?

Whistler

Beneath the highest altitude of the Rockies
I've stood, knowing these peaks would remain
Unfamiliar snow tops glistened as phenomena
Visible in the sultry August sun.

The Pomona Valley's hills were infants
To the great mammoths of the Colorado,
But as I drove through them each day,
Only heat linked me to their shadows.

Above California are three great relics,
Mt. Hood, Mt. Rainer, and the volcanic Mt. St. Helens.
In the Great Northwest they are places, not experiences yet,
I've not moved toward the beauty of their crescents.

But in the Canadian mountains I am tantalized.
They beckon me in and deceive me with their innocence.
Wildlife seeks me, I not them.
The wet cold breezes linger in June,
Offer late spring and early autumn in the same brisk air.
I awake and see the familiar moist clouds descend.
They dampen my hair as they drift lower,
And kiss the sage glass of the lake,
Moving into another day far in the Cascades.

Poems from Maui

1

Maui taught me
To discriminatively listen
To the difference
Between wooden planks
And the birds on paradise,
While the birds of paradise
Were audibly silent
They were visibly audible.
I learned that the ocean
Speaks with its own
Phonemic awareness
And the sky writes stories
With the clouds
And like a child
On a literary journey,
I listened to one, while
Reading the other.

2

Three pages of poetry snatched from my notebook
Into the Hawaiian air, blown across a beach on Maui.
Like naughty children, running here nor there
They baited me to chase,
I remained and watched,
Hoping perhaps they would stop.
But being notes, not kids,
As trade winds had another agenda,
They disappeared in the distance.
I thought,
Perhaps, the poems
Were intended for someone else.

3

I write long and hard,
Fingertips to keys.
Once words find subject matter
I'm awake
As my love partner slumbers,
Dreaming of nothing, so he says,
Which is puzzling, filled with dissonance.

I'm an anxious trumpet,
Waiting consonance,
Attempting to find meaning,
Writing long and hard,
Fingertips to keys,
Hoping for language
Someone will read.

For example,
On a plane to Maui with my sleeping lover
On the right and a sleepy stranger on left,
Each lost in comprehension.

Motivated me to write long and hard,
Right through dissension,
Realizing a lack of subject matter,
Didn't matter to them,
But it mattered to me.
Call it flight vulnerability,
But they were asleep,
So I wrote,
"Ripe fruit, white water, the right sunset,"
Ah, evidently the theme of next poem,
So it seemed,
As I write long and hard,
Fingertips to keys.

Warm Good-bye

Can I deny what I feel?
On a summer day,
Sitting under a maple tree,
Peering through the leaves,
A mosaic of blues and greens,
Farther away than me,
Still clinging to the earth
Exuding beauty and peace.

Can I deny what I see?
The same summer
Turning to autumn
Instead of winter to spring,
Flowers no longer vibrant,
Moths losing wings,
Grass fading brown,
Insects dazed on the ground.

Can I deny what I hear?
Once alluring sounds of mating,
Now the silence of separating,
Creatures leaving parents,
Fowl no longer spouses,
Only the ducks monogamous.
Can I just be mundane
And recite two adages?

"Nothing is forever"
"Everything must change."

Good-bye, sweet summer.

Sugar Break

No more sugar!
I'm not talking about
Duvie's Persian cat
With the mischievous grin,
Or my man's syrupy kisses,
Or molasses skin,
Nor the lady called Honey,
Instead of Ms. Sucrose.

Literally

Sugar no longer
Belongs in my mouth
You know that white crystal
Or powdery stuff,
I mean it; don't care
If it's raw, light, or dark,
I'm not interested
In organic derivatives,
Just the demarcation spaced
Between my waist and my hips.

Seattle's Summer Soup

Summer rain in Seattle
Is like living in a pot of broth
Inviting, healing vapors
Mixed in mist from clouds,
Soft breezes stirring damp leaves,
Floral petals, red bark steam,
Aroma of moist grassy soil
Poured in more showers
And the smell of water
Intensifies, mixed
With duck, salmon-turtle.

Poetic Reflections of Love

And then there was love …

My last poetic reflections are about what we all desire. Love reveals the importance of friends, family, and life, while providing a deeper meaning for who we are or who we have become. It was love that gave me the desire to share the poetic reflections in this book. These reflections convey some of my values, passions, and commitments, which are some of the elements that express the love that has been profound in my life. It is my hope that you have found love in your friends, family, and life; perhaps one day you may share those loving experiences through your own poetic reflections.

Husband

What's more pleasant
Than when you awake?
Tumble out of bed,
You stand,
Finding your footing
With arthritic knees,
Years of being a busy man
Too constant for our children,
Insisting they maintain purpose
No neglect in their eyes or mine.
Dependable,
Unrelentingly kind,
But stubborn in the ways
You felt were right.
Traditional stature,
Conventional in action,
Possible as your spouse to relax,
You were never missing
When it counted.
Your passion forever thick,
It glued me into a beautiful woman.
No way not to be with your kisses
On pregnant bellies,
Unshaved underarms,
Morning breath.
Leaving me breathless,
I have lived four lifetimes
Waiting for you to awake.
Gray whispers of dawn
When you didn't leave
But came.
Daybreaks with earnest concerns,
Sunlit rise that beckons exercise.
Resting in our empty nest,
Wherever a day reaches me,

I wait for you
And these times,
As you stumble
Ever so slightly,
Holding onto the bed frame,
I am thinking,
"What a man.
My God, What a Man!"

Honey Child

When I was out strolling without a care
A child ran past that smelled of licorice.
He made me think of my childhood sweetness
When candy stuck to my fingers and hair,
And I wondered,
If the fragrance in the air
Lingered with such sweet contentment.

Devotion

Walking hand in hand,
Looking over the smoky gray lake
Beneath the white morning sky
We felt the cool spring air
Beads above our lips,
Gifts from moving fast,
Discussing our pubescent past.
First campus home, young parents,
Staying romantic, empty nest,
Long partnership,
Memories we now celebrate.

Unnoticed, we came to that
Small familiar bridge
Necessary to cross
For our morning exercise.
We stopped, pleasantly surprised,
Our eyes greeted love
With ebony feathers
A trace of cherry red,
A blot of canary yellow,
The envy of any designer's thoughts.

One on the left, dining on seeds,
Gifts in tribute from other admirers,
And on the right railing, standing erect,
The mate singing in high trills to announce
Their presence.
So as not to disturb these birds,
We waited, feasting on the view,
As we respected their territory.

But as flawed creatures to time,
We acquiescence to the day's demands
And pulling up on our toes,
We moved forward slowly
With eyes downward in homage
As unwelcome guests, exhaling our breaths
Upon reaching the other side,
Thankful that these lovers were unmoved,
Steadfast in their purpose
And our understanding of devotion.

Arousal

I heard you whisper yes.
It was with a soft moan, slight twist,
A sleepy caress.
I think you knew
I was waiting for you.
I moved my fingers down your flesh,
Leaving tracks,
That went back
The other way
… So I did.

Renewal

Fill eyes with tears.
Feel tears in eyes,
To reprise,
The crescent act
Of flooding the
Fertile concave
While touching
The convex.
Let in rain,
Tears of thunder,
Tear asunder pain
From nescience
As awareness springs,
      Flourish!
As spring nourishes,
Love again.

My Fantasy

I seek to unwind the illusions of you.
Falling back to the reality of my previous love,
Safe, perfect, permanent for who I am,
Go away, stay where you belong,
Out of this time and space
You are only in my mind,
Nowhere else.
You could never penetrate
The great divide.

A Hymn for Him

Sensibilities are not always feminine,
Sometimes, they smell of musk,
Which is anything but a lady.
But when they are kind and sweet,
The fragrance is endearing.

By the Lake

The lake is where
I wait for you.
Peering down
Into endless depths
Of emptiness.
Is there nothing to be found?
I need to know
How deep is your love
And I will tell you
How wide is mine.
I cannot swim to safety
Without your hand
Reaching for me.
We must save each other
During this turbulent time.

Voice

I found my voice today.
I had no choice.
It was standing behind me, smiling.
I just turned and said, "Hello."
I can't wait until tomorrow.
My voice I may follow.

A Privacy Screen

I bought twelve arborvitaes
To provide a privacy screen,
Preventing curious neighbors
From achieving
What they're seeking:
Invading private dreams,
Napping,
Meditating,
Praying,
Intimacy.

One dozen 10-foot shrubs,
Tall enough to do the job,
High enough to conceal,
The voyeurs' view,
A tangible chore,
fait accompli!

Now, how to hide
From a lover's eyes,
Searching my intangible plea,
Too close proximity
For me,
Perhaps, I need
More trees?

Poetry

You believed it was abandonment
But wasn't it you that really left?
Too fickle to be continuous
Until you discovered
You wanted me back.
So I just waited.

A Request

Can you love me for me,
Not for you?
Even though I love me
For you,
And love you for you,
Can you love me
Unconditionally?
I've tried, but you keep
Coming in first.

Whispers to Scream

Have you ever loved?
From whispers to scream,
Whispers with lips next to your ear
Asking, "What's your name?"
Whispers of nervous sighs
Asking, "Will you be mine?"
Soft liquid whispers in the
Small of the neck,
Uttering, "I'll want you forever,"
Attached to passion,
Conversations of dedication,
Talks of monogamy,
Eventually, monotony.
Meat or fish,
Who'll wash the dish?
Boredom leads to dissatisfaction,
Distractions to other attractions,
Trust turns to mistrust,
Truth to lies,
Raised voices
Of guilty alibis.
What seemed
Your love whispers,
Are now
One's SCREAM!

A Finite Unit

One step took me
A thousand miles from where
I stood, and I saw for the first time,
The end of where I've been.
I knew it was over;
Alas, it was over.
As you cried
And I tried
Never to give up like the others,
But the good memories
Are smudged carbon copies
And the tears no longer real
Just big fat crocodiles
Made of pretentious liquid
And our passion
An unromantic end.

Umoja Means Unity

I saw an infant
Carrying an infant
The other day.
The first infant,
Only four feet tall,
Perhaps thirteen, maybe younger
Pudgy round,
Cute with a ponytail ball.
The other infant,
"Now here's the rub,"
Laid against
The cute infant's chest.
Waking and dozing
At an Umoja fest.
This infant even cuter!
Let's say,
nineteen inches long.
Napping
In the hot August sun.
The older infant too young
And the younger infant
Much too young
To assess own needs
Food, water, an umbrella
And I,
Too much a stranger
To intervene.
For three hours,
Cute and Cuter strolled,
I watched,
As guardian angel
With no control.
Frustrated at times,
Even desperate,
Accepting the respectable fate
That no matter the ages,
These two infants,
Mama and child were inseparable.

Song for My Sisters

Kiss her in the mirror,
She's the one you should cherish.
She will love you unconditionally;
Love that fulfills and completes you.

Kiss her in the mirror, my sisters
And love the one who can raise your
Daughters to be survivors and
Sons to be "true lovers."

Kiss the one who will make you
Believe in God when there are no others.
For she is the one who will discern
Passionate virtue from reckless desires.

She is the one, who will say, "Enough," "No,"
"Unacceptable," and mean it. Because
Her mother, sister, and daughter are watching
Her reflection as they polish their own.

She is in love, in love with the very essence of you,
And will show your lover how to love you back.
Did *his* mother kiss her mirror, no matter?
Allow him to find you kissing yours, and he will
Know what to do and so will you.

So sisters go to that private place, take a long, lingering
Look in the mirror, move closer and closer,
For she is you and you are she,
Say those three words, you give to the one most dear,
"I Love You," slowly close your beautiful eyes,
Pucker your moist lovely lips; now kiss her!
She is the only one you will ever kiss
Who will dry your tears,
All your days on this earth.

Walking Still

I'm walking still,
Even as I dodge
A big fat polyp,
Bleeding trouble,
Elderly father,
Brokenhearted,
Physically twisted,
Brave young woman,
Running strong
In wheelchair.

I'm walking still,
Some days with my
Lungs underfoot
And others with
Foot in mouth.
Can't conceive
How I became so lost,
Loving too much of me
And not enough of
Others.

I'm walking still,
Still trying, still trying,
Each time, trying
To walk right.
Still walking,
Head up,
Hands down,
Eyes forward,
Ears open.

I'm walking still,
Cause I can't
Lie down.

Your Poetic Reflections

Your Poetic Reflections

Your Poetic Reflections

Your Poetic Reflections

Your Poetic Reflections

Your Poetic Reflections

Printed in the United States
by Baker & Taylor Publisher Services

Printed in the United States
by Baker & Taylor Publisher Services